"'Clothed with Christ': Wh .... just a metaphor. It's what we are given for our security before God now and the dazzling finery of the Wedding Feast of the Lamb. Let Brian Thomas show you Christ's wardrobe!"

—Michael Horton,
Professor of Theology,
Westminster Seminary California and
co-host of the White Horse Inn podcast.

"In this practical guide for Christian living, Pastor Thomas shows sinners how to live the baptismal life—daily putting off the tattered rags of their own righteousness and putting on the righteousness and holiness of Jesus who by their baptism into his death and resurrection gives them his own risen life to live in this dying world."

—Harold L. Senkbeil,
Author of *The Care of Souls*,
Lexham Press, 2019

"Brian W. Thomas' masterful *Clothed with Christ* is an essential read for anyone seeking to understand the profound biblical metaphor of clothing as it relates to our spiritual lives. With deep theological insight and engaging narrative, Thomas guides us through the Scriptures, unveiling how the theme of clothing shapes our understanding of sin, salvation, and sanctification. This book brilliantly stitches together the narrative of redemption with the threads of righteousness, justice, and love, weaving a tapestry that displays the beauty of being spiritually dressed by Christ. It's a compelling invitation to embrace the gospel's transformative power, which covers our shame and adorns us in Christ's righteousness, making it a must-read for both believers and seekers of truth."

—Justin S. Holcomb,
Bishop of the Episcopal Diocese
of Central Florida, author,
and seminary professor

"Such a creative piece of work this is! In *Clothed with Christ*, Brian Thomas pulls on one of Scripture's strongest but most overlooked threads—that of clothing—and weaves something undeniably fresh, deeply pastoral, and just plain interesting out of it. Puns all very much intended. Thomas has given us a whole new lens through which to view not only the outfits we wear each day but the Gospel itself. Highly recommended."

—David Zahl,
author of *Low Anthropology*
and *Seculosity*

"This beautifully written book is a splendid example of how, from the opening of Genesis to the closing of Revelation, Christ is preached to us in a rich variety of ways. Brian Thomas invites us into the biblical wardrobe, where the regal robes of Jesus cover our shameful nakedness. These pages will make you think, make you laugh, and make you shout for joy over the gifts of Christ, who has decked us out like kings and queens. We wear the very best; we wear Jesus!"

—Chad Bird,
Scholar-in-Residence, 1517

CLOTHED WITH CHRIST

A BIBLICAL STYLE GUIDE FOR SINNERS

BRIAN WILLIAM THOMAS

CLOTHED WITH CHRIST

A BIBLICAL STYLE GUIDE FOR SINNERS

FOREWORD BY ROBERT M. HILLER

Clothed with Christ: A Biblical Style Guide for Sinners

Published by:
1517 Publishing
PO Box 54032
Irvine, CA 92619-4032

Publisher's Cataloging-In-Publication Data
(Prepared by Cassidy Cataloguing, Inc.)

Names: Thomas, Brian W. (Brian William), 1972- author. | Hiller, Robert M., writer of foreword.
Title: Clothed with Christ : a biblical style guide for sinners / Brian W. Thomas ; foreword by Robert M. Hiller.
Description: Irvine, CA : 1517 Publishing, [2024] | Includes bibliographical references and index.
Identifiers: ISBN: 978-1-956658-92-7 (paperback) | 978-1-956658-93-4 (ebook) | 978-1-964419-07-7 (audio)
Subjects: LCSH: Biblical costume. | Clothing and dress—Biblical teaching. | Fashion—Religious aspects— Christianity. | Sin. | Salvation. | Jesus Christ—Presence. | God (Christianity) | BISAC: RELIGION / Christian Theology / General. | RELIGION / Christian Living / General. | RELIGION / Christian Living / Spiritual Growth.
Classification: LCC: BS680.C65 T46 2024 | DDC: 241.674—dc23

Printed in the United States of America.

Cover art by Zachariah James Stuef.

For Rachel

Contents

Foreword

Years ago on *Late Night*, David Letterman had a delightfully awkward interview with Anna Wintour, the muse for Miranda Priestly, the so-named devil in *The Devil Wears Prada*. The interview took place in 2009, when many people in the United States were reeling on the heels of an economic crisis. Letterman asked her what she would say to those who cannot afford to buy the designer outfits in her fashion magazine. The back and forth is classic Letterman.

Letterman: On a budget of subsistence living, can you still appear fashionable?

Wintour: Of course! What is wonderful about fashion today is that it is available to so many different people at so many different prices...

Letterman: Say a person used to have $100 in their fashion budge—and lord knows I don't know anybody who has a fashion budget—but they used to have $100 in their fashion budget and now they only have $20 in their fashion budget. How do you do that on twenty bucks?

Wintour: They can buy lipstick.[1]

I mean, let them eat cake while they are at it! Wintour's ambivalence was both embarrassing and insulting. At least if

---

[1] Letterman, "Anna Wintour on the Accuracy of 'The Devil Wears Prada'," YouTube Video, 10:12, February 1, 2022, https://www.youtube.com/watch?v=viTU747i6r8.

you are cutting costs at the grocery store, your lips can still look luxurious!

Here is someone whose magazine is responsible for guiding fashion and telling people how they should dress, but who has no clue what they can afford to wear. It seems to me that if someone is going to take the responsibility to tell us how to dress, they should at least know what we can afford to buy!

It strikes me how very different this attitude is from that of our Lord Jesus. Throughout the scriptures, our spiritual condition is described in terms of clothing. Given that our sinfulness has left us spiritually impoverished, without a dime to our name, we have nothing with which to purchase for ourselves any sort of clothing to cover our sin-exposed bodies. The Lord Jesus knows this. He knows our poverty. He knows our sin. He knows all of it. He finds us, cold, naked, and alone, shivering in the dark with no means by which we can cover ourselves.

But, Jesus, you see, is no devil in Prada, demanding that impoverished sinners give money they do not have to wear clothes they cannot afford. Rather, he takes matters into his own hands, clothing naked and guilty sinners with his own righteousness! He removes his garments and puts them on you. He enters your poverty and takes your nakedness and guilt all the way to the cross. In exchange, he covers you with his clothing—clothing of the royal King of Heaven and Earth—so that you may enter the King's banquet to be treated like royalty! To be sure, he demands you dress appropriately to enter his Father's presence. But, fear not, for he's given you the clothes to put on. He designed them and purchased them with his own blood for you!

My friend Brian Thomas is a pastor who has been trained in the fashion school of this saving Gospel. In this delightful book, he demonstrates his awareness of how our spiritual poverty results in lives that are naked on account of sin and vainly clothed with filthy rags. Pastor Thomas shows us that the only answer to our plight is not found in buying what we cannot afford, but in the shed blood of Jesus Christ! With keen theological insight, each chapter of the book thus clothes us in the baptismal reality St. Paul proclaims to us when he writes, "For as many of you as were baptized into Christ have put on Christ" (Gal 3:27). Jesus Christ alone can cover your sin and shame. And He has done it!

I pray this little book will drive you to rejoice in the fact that, though the devil may wear Prada, the Lord Jesus Christ wears your sins and clothes you in his own righteousness! May you know better what it means to be clothed in Christ!

Bob Hiller
Senior Pastor, Community Lutheran Church
Escondido/San Marcos, California

Introduction

Tracing a Golden Thread

I will greatly rejoice in the Lord; my soul shall exult
in my God, for he has clothed me with the garments
of salvation; he has covered me with the robe of
righteousness, as a bridegroom decks himself like
a priest with a beautiful headdress, and as a bride
adorns herself with her jewels.
—Isaiah 61:10

My mother owned a hair salon when I was growing up. I
spent countless hours after school doing homework, sweeping hair, and washing/folding white towels. Like most salons,
there were plenty of fashion magazines stocked in the waiting
area. From *Vogue*, *InStyle*, and *Cosmopolitan,* I learned to
appreciate the work of Coco Chanel, Yves St. Laurent, and
Oscar de la Renta. Additionally, my grandmother lived down
the street. She had worked at one of the original Levi's plants
sewing jeans and jackets as a young woman, so she was an
adept seamstress, often making clothes for her grandchildren, especially "yours truly," who was often a difficult and

opinionated customer. The combination of these experiences piqued my interest in fashion at an early age. In fact, I was voted "most fashionable" in my high school yearbook. This was in the 1980s, so if flashbacks of pegged jeans, spiky hair, and Duran Duran come to mind, you wouldn't be far off.

Ralph Waldo Emerson once said, "Being perfectly well-dressed gives one a tranquility that no religion can bestow." I certainly enjoy being well-dressed, but I beg to differ. An often overlooked but important fashion motif runs through the Bible like a golden thread from Genesis to Revelation. As the prophet Isaiah rejoices in the passage cited above, being "clothed" by God serves as an image of salvation. It dresses up the doctrine of justification by grace alone through faith alone for the sake of Christ alone, providing a true tranquility that *only* Christ can bestow.

My purpose in writing this little book is to trace the thread of this motif in order to appreciate the lengths to which God has gone to style sinners with his Son's righteous robes. In doing so, I hope you will be comforted by a spirituality that keeps its focus on Christ the Master Tailor for sinners who would otherwise stand naked and ashamed.

Chapter 1

Naked

And the man and his wife were both naked and
were not ashamed.
—Genesis 2:25

When my daughters were young, they loved the *Madeline* books by Ludwig Bemelmans. The orphanage teacher, Miss Clavel, captures the universal knowledge of the human condition in the following scene:

> In the middle of the night
> Miss Clavel turned on the light
> and said, "Something is not right!"[1]

While not everyone agrees with the biblical account of human origins, you would be hard-pressed to find someone who would argue with Miss Clavel's assessment. Our sense of

---

[1] Ludwig Bemelmans, *Madeline* (New York: Penguin, 1977), 17.

justice demands an explanation. Something is definitely not right—not right with the world, not right with other people, not right with ourselves. The Bible refers to this *not rightness* as sin. But it was not always that way.

In the beginning, God looked across the vast beauty of all that he had made and confessed that it was "very good" (Gen 1:31). All was good but one thing. The man was all alone. Thus, God created a perfect match for him. Adam and Eve are portrayed as the crowning glory of God's creative work, reflecting the image and likeness of their Creator, which includes both unity and diversity, equality and uniqueness. A man and woman are bound together in a loving marital union where two become "one flesh" (Gen 2:24).

The intimacy of this relationship is expressed with two Hebrew words: *àrommin* and *yitbosheshu*. They are "naked" and "unashamed." Two words that now seem incongruous even for those who are in the best of physical shape and emotional stability. The couple's nakedness is not merely a description of their primeval nature but a profound theological statement. Nakedness equals innocence. We know this because they do not remain in such a blissful state for long.

In *Paradise Lost*, Milton speaks of clothing as "troublesome disguises that we wear."[2] The need to disguise or cover up is only necessary when you have something to hide. Nakedness expresses a lack of concealment. The couple has no fear of exposure. Each is completely transparent to the other without even a hint of embarrassment. They know one another in every possible sense, because they are without shame. Thus, the first time that shame is mentioned in Scripture is to celebrate its absence.

Possessing an unfaltering identity as God's children, they were at one with God, at one with each other, and at one with the creation they were called to steward through

---

[2]   John Milton, *Paradise Lost*, Book IV, line 739. Public Domain.

their vocations. Clothing was not only optional, it was unnecessary. They could look upon one another clear-eyed and in perfect freedom—a freedom from shame because they had done nothing in thought, word, or deed to be ashamed of.

Unclothed and unabashed. Such thoughts seem foreign, especially for those of us who are self-conscious even when fully dressed. As I write this, I have an annual physical in a few weeks that I am dreading. I do not enjoy being naked and exposed, even to my doctor who sees nakedness every day. It's called an examining room for a reason, and who enjoys having their physical, emotional, or spiritual life laid bare? Yet deep down, I believe everyone longs to be totally naked—completely known and completely loved. Everyone craves honest and vulnerable relationships without fear of judgment.

Such was life in paradise, where the image of God in humanity reflected peace and purity. Simultaneous exposure and lack of shame summarize the goodness of God's creation and the relationships he created. Everything was beautiful. Everything was right! The key word being *was*. Past tense. What went wrong? To read the second chapter of Genesis brings an understanding of what humanity has lost.

SHREWD TO NUDE

> Now the serpent was more crafty than any other
> beast of the field that the Lord God had made.
> —Genesis 3:1

The second act of a traditional five-act play brings conflict, something that needs resolution to ensure a happily ever after. And this is what we find in the biblical drama of Genesis 3—a story referred to as "the fall," where God's perfect world becomes corrupted by sin. Eugene Peterson's description of sin's entrance into God's good world is not an overstatement: "A catastrophe has occurred. We are no longer in continuity with our good beginning. We have been separated from it by a disaster. We are also, of course, separated from our good end. We are, in other words, in the middle of a mess."[3]

As the narrative transitions to the second act, the writer deftly brings together the innocent nakedness of the happy couple with the craftiness of the deceitful serpent. By using a creative play on words, the scene has set the stage for temptation and disobedience. The couple is *àrommin* (smooth skinned) in Genesis 2:25, but the serpent is *àrum* (smooth talking) in Genesis 3:1. From nude to shrewd, the tempter enters the garden sanctuary to cast doubt on God's prohibition and promise by enticing Adam and Eve to be autonomous equals with God: "You will not die. For God knows that when you eat of it your eyes will be opened, and you will be like God, knowing good and evil" (Gen 3:4-5).

William McDavid makes a helpful comparison between the serpent's conversation with Eve and that of a man trying to lure a married woman into an illicit affair.

> Imagine a married woman, totally happy with her life, content, who has never imagined infidelity because she cannot conceive of life outside her marriage. But then someone asks, "are you *really* married?" Suddenly a new set of possibilities—with their attendant temptations—might open up to her.[4]

---

[3] Eugene Peterson, *Working the Angels: The Shape of Pastoral Integrity* (Grand Rapids: Eerdmans, 1993), 82.

[4] William McDavid, *Eden and Afterward: A Mockingbird Guide to Genesis* (Charlottesville, VA: Mockingbird Ministries, 2014), 16.

The serpent cleverly inserts a new possibility of self-suffi-
ciency apart from God. Thus, the sudden appeal of the tree
to Eve's sense and sensibility, "So when the woman saw that
the tree was good for food, and that it was a delight to the
eyes, and that the tree was to be desired to make one wise,
she took of its fruit and ate, and she also gave some to her
husband who was with her, and he ate" (Gen 3:6). McDavid
concludes:

> The person about to cheat on their spouse doesn't conceive
> of it as evil, but as some kind of good—a way to avoid resent-
> ing their husband, or a pursuit of what seems like genuine
> love, or a response to boredom, the need to inject meaning
> into a stagnant life. It is only at some point during the affair
> that the knowledge that things are now askew will hit like a
> ton of bricks. Whatever moral implications of wrongdoing
> there may be only becomes totally clear after the fact.[5]

The serpent's prediction rings true at first pass. The
couple did not immediately drop dead after eating from the
tree of the knowledge of good and evil. But something *in*
them and *between* them did die—spiritually and relationally.
The couple remains *àrommin*, but it is no longer praisewor-
thy. Consider Adam's response to God's rhetorical question,
"I heard the sound of you in the garden, and I was afraid,
because I was *naked*, and I hid myself" (Gen 3:10). Their
eyes are opened and from here on nakedness will serve as
a symbol of shame, driving their relationship apart as they
blame-shift rather than take responsibility for their actions.[6]

What is true for Adam and Eve is true for us all because
their story describes the state of humanity. In their rebellious

---

[5]   Ibid., 17.
[6]   See also Genesis 9:22-23; Isaiah 47:3; Ezekiel 16:37, and Revelation 16:15.

ascension to be "like God" we discover something universal: shame as a result of guilt, self-vindication instead of confession, conflict instead of peace, and the struggle for domination through manipulation across the spectrum of human experience. Ultimately, we find death instead of life. Paradoxically, death reigns in the midst of life. Like Adam and Eve, we become the walking dead.

The image of God that previously reflected *shalom* has been broken, and the cracks of that brokenness have spread to all humanity. Thomas Cranmer captured this post-fall anthropology when he wrote, "What the heart loves, the will chooses, and the mind justifies." Such was the case with Adam and Eve; such is the case with you and me.

This story is a vivid portrait of the human condition: we are created in God's image, yet we all have chosen to sin because we are all sinners; therefore, we all are in need of salvation, for "all have sinned and fallen short of the glory of God" (Rom 3:23). Thankfully, nakedness is not the last word of the story.

Chapter 2

An Unconventional Materials Challenge

And they sewed fig leaves together and made
themselves loincloths.
—Genesis 3:7

For many years, I enjoyed the reality television show *Project Runway,* where aspiring fashion designers compete through a variety of challenges testing their creative and technical merit. My favorite episode each season was called the "unconventional materials challenge." Instead of sourcing fabric from a traditional textile shop, the contestants are taken to places like a hardware store or a candy shop to select atypical materials with which to create couture garments. The more imaginative the designers are, the more likely they will win the approval of the judges on the runway.

While this may work for reality TV, it does not when it comes to the reality of God's judgment. The consequence of Adam and Eve's fall is marked by alienation. Immediately, they attempt a game of hide-and-seek from an omniscient God, clothing themselves with fig leaves—the first unconventional materials challenge failure.

Shame is the result of a guilty conscience, the awareness that something is not right. There was nothing wrong with their naked bodies, rather, they were now self-conscious of their nakedness, a sign of how helpless and vulnerable they had become. Clothing thus forms a symbolic barrier to protect us from exposure to others in a dangerous world cut off from God and estranged from one another.

St. Paul tells us that God has written his law upon our hearts, and our conscience serves to either accuse or excuse our behavior (Rom 2:15). In a rather sardonic essay against morality, Mark Twain becomes an unlikely ally of the apostle when he calls humanity the only "animal that blushes," a creature who is forced to clothe himself because he is the only one who possesses a sense of shame or morality.[1]

While guilt and shame go hand-in-hand, they are not the same. Guilt is a forensic term from the courtroom. When one is measured by the standard of law and found guilty, it matters little if the defendant feels the weight of his crime. When the verdict is pronounced, a person is declared either not guilty or guilty. Guilt is, therefore, the objective culpability for transgressing legal boundaries. Shame is the subjective emotional consequence, and one that we don't always handle so well.

When God asks Adam, "Who told you that you were naked?," it wasn't because he lacked the information. He graciously sought out the couple to get an admission of guilt, clearly evidenced by their fig leaf faux pas. Adam's response can be likened to a toddler who answers "no" to

---

[1] Samuel Clemens, "The Damned Human Race," *The American Tradition in Literature*, Vol. 2, eds. George and Barbara Perkins (New York: McGraw-Hill, 1985), 493.

his mother through chocolate-stained lips when asked if he ate the cookie. Instead of accepting responsibility through repentance and confession, he exacerbates it by becoming defensive, and indirectly impugns God in the process.

WHAT NOT TO WEAR

The Italian clothing designer Miuccia Prada once said that "fashion is instant language." The instant language that fig leaves communicate is self-justification. Spiritually speaking, this was the definitive "what not to wear" scenario. We may be able to "control the narrative" or hide our flaws from one another, but not so with God. Our fig leaves are see-through mesh before his all-seeing eyes.

In Jean-Paul Sartre's book *Being and Nothingness*, there is a chapter called "The Look," where he explores the relationship between self-consciousness and shame. He tells a story of a man who is secretly peeping through the keyhole of his neighbor's door, lost in the voyeuristic delight of being in the know until he hears the floor creak behind him and comes to the startling realization that someone else is watching him through another keyhole. He has been caught looking, and now finds himself embarrassed to be the object of someone else's observation.

Though Sartre remained an atheist, he was on to something we intuitively grasp. To be known is to be vulnerable. You are no longer autonomous. You are now bound by someone else's knowledge of you. As a result, an unsettling question arises: What will he do with the information he has discovered?

When we expand Sartre's existentialist experiment to include God as the observer, it becomes frightening, as the writer to the Hebrews makes clear: "And no creature is hidden from His sight, but all are naked and exposed to the eyes of Him to whom we must give account" (Heb 4:13). Who wants to stand under God's almighty gaze when you know you are guilty of high treason? The fight-or-flight response kicks in—and since we are no match for an omnipotent God, we enlist ourselves into a sinner's witness protection program and run for cover.

King David asks a relevant question in Psalm 139:7–8 and provides a troublesome answer for those who want to follow Adam and Eve into hiding:

> Where shall I go from your Spirit?
> Or where shall I flee from your presence?
> If I ascend to heaven, you are there!
> If I make my bed in Sheol, you are there!

God is everywhere present. Where do we go when the route of evasion proves impossible? We could close our eyes and delude ourselves into believing that God does not exist (atheism). But I have found that denial is simply another form of prevarication, and it will do nothing to satisfy our objective guilt and resultant shame in the long run. To be honest, it will only magnify it and lead to the further suppression of the truth in unrighteousness.[2]

Another popular alternative is to appeal the guilty verdict by defending ourselves. And rather ironically, the primary way we have historically attempted do so is through religion. We try to cover ourselves with the fig leaves of piety, where we convince ourselves that if we sew enough good works together, it will tip the scale of God's justice in our favor. But as we trace this course of action throughout the Bible, we find rather quickly that the garments of religion do little to hide our sin. In fact, they only make matters worse,

---

[2] See Romans 1:18–32.

because we start to believe that we have the power to save ourselves. We even create religious catchphrases like, "God helps those who help themselves," that sound spiritual but are definitively not![3]

Like Adam and Eve, we fall for the lie of the serpent and think that we, too, can shortcut our way to "become like God." The prophet Isaiah responds to such foolishness with a hard truth: "All our righteous deeds are like menstrual rags" before a holy God (Isa 64:6). It will require a master tailor to cover up the mess we have made.

GARMENTS OF GRACE

> And the Lord God made for Adam and for his wife
> garments of skins and clothed them.
> —Genesis 3:21

After experiencing a treasonous coup in his garden sanctuary, it is surprising that God does not wipe humanity out and start over. Instead, he seeks out the self-justifying couple and provides a promise to redeem the world, one that is carefully threaded through the serpent's curse:

> I will put enmity between you and the woman,
> and between your offspring and her offspring;
> he shall bruise your head,
> and you shall bruise his heel.

This pronouncement from Genesis 3:15 is the first gospel promise in the Bible. Bruce Waltke explains:

---

[3]   The medieval equivalent during Martin Luther's day was "do what is within you to do" (*facere quod in se est*).

Though Eve deserves only death, God does not turn His back on her. Instead, in His kindness God restores her through the mission of her seed. His purpose will not be defeated. Humankind will yet be crowned with glory and honor, bringing all things under their feet as God originally intended.[4]

Adam subsequently names his wife Eve, which means "life," demonstrating faith in God's promised hope for humanity. While Adam and Eve's fig leaf foolishness is firmly rejected, they are not. Out of a profound love for them and their progeny, the divine stylist provides an appropriate covering for their nakedness—the skin of an animal—foreshadowing the sacrifice of that promised Seed: "the very Lamb of God who takes away the sin of the world" (John 1:29).

Martin Luther notes how their new clothes will serve as a visible catechism to remind them of their mortality (Law) and their coming Messiah (Gospel):

> Here Adam and Eve are dressed in garments by the Lord Himself. Whenever they looked at their garments, these were to serve as a reminder to them to give thought to their wretched fall from supreme happiness into the utmost misfortune and trouble. Thus they were to be constantly afraid of sinning, to repent continuously, and to sigh for the forgiveness of sins through the promised Seed. This is also why He clothed them, not in foliage or in cotton but in the skins of slain animals, for a sign that they are mortal and that they are living in certain death.[5]

---

[4]   Bruce Waltke, *An Old Testament Theology: An exegetical, canonical, and thematic approach,* (Grand Rapids: Zondervan, 2007), 266.
[5]   LW 1:221.

We learn two important truths from this covering. First, God is the only one who can style sinners. Second, the fabric God selects to cover our shame is not cheap. It costs the life of another. The biblical doctrines of substitutionary atonement and justification by grace through faith are interwoven Good News for sinners who turn in faith to the One who is gracious, slow to anger, and abounding in steadfast love for his creation.

Chapter 5

The Champion's Jersey

Blessed is the one whose transgression is forgiven,
whose sin is covered.
—Psalm 32:1

When my youngest daughter was twelve, she served as
the manager of her junior high basketball team. I don't
know if you've ever had the pleasure of seeing seventh and
eighth grade girls play basketball, but I liken it to watching Mike Tyson compete in a spelling bee: it's awkward,
difficult, and yet a little entertaining. During one game, a
girl on the opposing team committed five fouls within the
first five minutes, resulting in disqualification and being
benched for the remainder of the game. In other words, she
contributed nothing to her team's eventual victory except
her error.

The girl who came off the bench to replace her, how-
ever, was extraordinary. She followed the rules of the game
and put so many points on the board by halftime that her
team's lead was insurmountable. Without a doubt, she was

the game's MVP. As a pastor in the bleachers, I found this
to be a useful illustration for understanding our salvation
in Jesus Christ. Surprisingly, my daughter did not find it as
cool as I did on the car ride home, since her team just lost.

If guilt and shame are not covered by our fig leaves,
how then does God ultimately cover us with his garments of
grace while remaining holy and just? After all, a good judge
does not turn a blind eye to injustice.

The law of God is good and holy. It expresses God's will
and tells us what we should and should not do. The problem
is not with the law but with our inability to keep it in thought,
word, and deed—perfectly, consistently, and entirely. Thus,
the primary purpose of the law is to expose sin for what it is
and lead us to the Savior God has provided (Gal 3:24). Said
differently, everyone has fouled out of the game of life and
must ride the bench because of sin.

There is no way to escape our disqualification, and
thus, there is no path to victory on our own. Self-help may
be a popular section of your local book store, but it is off
the table entirely when it comes to our standing before
a holy God. For that, we must rely upon someone else.
Rod Rosenbladt summarizes our personal and collective
problem:

> Apart from a God-given, Law-satisfying mediator, everyone
> of us stands before the righteous God as guilty and justly
> condemned by his just Law. *Someone* is going to have to
> satisfy divine justice, but we have not done so. Nor can we
> do so. *Someone* is going to have to pay the penalty for our
> sin, but we cannot pay it. We are part of the problem, not
> part of the solution.[1]

---

[1] Rod Rosenbladt, *Christ Alone* (Irvine, CA: New Reformation Publications, 2015), 21.

St. Paul provides the only solution:

> For all who rely on works of the law are under a curse; for
> it is written, "Cursed be everyone who does not abide by all
> things written in the Book of the Law, and do them." Now it
> is evident that no one is justified before God by the law, for
> "The righteous shall live by faith." But the law is not of faith,
> rather "The one who does them shall live by them." Christ
> redeemed us from the curse of the law by becoming a curse
> for us—for it is written, "Cursed is everyone who is hanged
> on a tree"—so that in Christ Jesus the blessing of Abraham
> might come to the Gentiles, so that we might receive the
> promised Spirit through faith. (Gal 3:10–14)

What we failed to do, Jesus accomplished through his perfect
life, death, and resurrection. He redeemed you from the curse
of the law by becoming a curse for you. Take a moment to
cherish those last two words, *for you*, for they beautifully
express the doctrine of substitutionary atonement.

Born under the law, Jesus satisfied every demand of the
law through his perfect life and innocent suffering. He didn't
abolish the law; he fulfilled it on your behalf.[2] By entering the
playing field in his incarnation, Jesus not only played the perfect game, but he also assumed the penalty for every foul ever
committed by humanity on the cross. He was stripped naked
in shame, so that you could stand clothed and unashamed.
Coco Chanel famously said, "The best things in life are free.
The second best are very expensive." She's right, of course.
But the righteous clothing God covers us with is uniquely
both—free and expensive. It is free to us, but it cost Jesus
everything.[3]

---

[2]   Matthew 5:17.
[3]   1 Peter 1:18.

The law, therefore, does not get the final word. Jesus takes our curse and delivers the cure by "imputing" to us his righteousness. This idea comes from the field of accounting, and means to credit something to another's account. Our salvation involves a two-way imputation.

First, God imputes our guilt and shame to Jesus as if he had committed our sins himself, and thus, he bears our death sentence, for the "wages of sin is death" (Rom 6:23). This is what makes Good Friday so very good—at least for you and me. As my professor, Rod Rosenbladt, often said in class, "The only thing you contribute to your salvation is your sin."

Second, God imputes Christ's righteousness to us, regarding us as if we had played the game of life perfectly. Luther referred to this as an "alien righteousness" because it comes from another. By nature, no one can claim to be righteous, but God declares it so for the sake of his righteous Son. Justification is a term borrowed from the courtroom to pronounce a verdict of "not guilty." Thus the Gospel gives what the Law requires—a righteous standing before a holy God.

In this twofold transaction, God's integrity is upheld as sin is fully punished. This is why God is able to remain "just and the justifier of the one who has faith in Jesus" (Rom 3:26).

PLAYING DRESS-UP IN CHRIST'S CLOSET

Designer Kate Spade once quipped, "Playing dress-up begins at age five and never truly ends." When children play dress-up, it often involves the assumption of another's identity that they are not qualified to bear. For example, my grandfather was a retired navy chief. He had a guest room that displayed his naval medals and mementos along with pictures of every ship on which he served in a thirty year career. My brother and I loved raiding his closet and dressing up in his old uniforms, pretending we were sailors fighting enemies in the South Pacific. If it helps, my grandfather had the documentary *Victory at Sea* running on a continuous loop for most of my childhood.

Playing dress-up is innocent fun for children. But there's an important difference when it comes to being clothed with Christ. When God the Father looks at us, he sees us as his sons because we are covered by his Son, though we have done nothing to merit or qualify for that filial status. Instead of pretending to be his children, we truly are his children by virtue of his adopting Word grasped through the gift of faith, apart from works of the law.

Think of faith like an outstretched hand taking hold of the gracious garments God has provided. When an anxious jailer asked Paul and Silas, "What must I do to be saved?," they answered, "Believe in the Lord Jesus" (Acts 16:30). The saving work had already been accomplished for the jailer with nothing more to be done; he was simply to trust that it was so *for him*. Gerhard Forde notes the passive nature of this saving gift:

> The faith by which one is justified is not an active verb of which the Old Adam or Eve is the subject; it is a state-of-being verb. Faith is the state of being grasped by the unconditional claim and promise of the God who calls into being that which is from that which is not. Faith means now having to deal with life in those terms.[4]

What life in those terms means is death and resurrection— dying to the old, naked self in Adam and living by faith in the new identity God has graciously clothed us with in Christ.

---

[4] Gerhard Forde, *Justification by Faith: A Matter of Death and Life* (Philadelphia: Fortress, 1982), 22.

And this takes us full circle. The poor girl who fouled out in the first quarter was delivered by the performance of the one who took her place. Though she sat passively on the bench, she nevertheless won the victory alongside her teammates, wearing the same jersey as the game's MVP.

In like manner, when St. John was given a vision of heaven, he saw the saints gathered around the throne of the Lamb of God wearing the white robes of their victorious champion (Rev 6:11; 19:8). Their debt has been forgiven; they are blessed because it is covered. It feels good to be on a winning team, even when everyone on that team has done nothing to earn that victory except for One.

Chapter 4

All Dressed in White

The only available candidates for matrimony are,
every last one of them, sinners.
—Robert Farrar Capon

One of my favorite moments of a wedding is the look of antic-ipation on the groom's face as the narthex doors open to reveal his bride, radiant in her wedding gown as she walks down the aisle to join him on the adventure called Holy Matrimony. Most brides have been dreaming of this day since they were little girls, and much of that dreaming centered on what they were going to wear. Whether she selects an A-line, jewel, trumpet, sheath, mermaid, or tea-length gown, one thing is certain—she wants to look beautiful, especially in the eyes of her beloved.

The Bible begins and ends with weddings. Adam and Eve are joined together in marital union in the garden, reveal-ing marriage as part of God's purpose for humanity from the start. History will close with the marriage celebration of Christ to his church—earthly marriage being fulfilled in the heavenly, demonstrating the eternal nature of this blessed estate.[1] Between these bookends, the most intimate way the Bible portrays the relationship of God to sinners is through the lens of marriage.

In the Old Testament, God loves Israel as a faithful husband despite the fact that she is often whoring after the gods of neighboring nations. Perhaps the most striking example of this is found in the prophet Hosea, whose life functions as an image of God's steadfast love. Hosea is commanded to marry a prostitute named Gomer, whose promiscuous nature symbolizes Israel's infidelity. Hosea remains faithful, seeking after Gomer just as God remains true to his beloved but faithless people. Instead of abandoning her, he romantically seeks her out and makes the following promise:

> And I will betroth you to me forever. I will betroth you to me in righteousness and in justice, in steadfast love and in mercy. I will betroth you to me in faithfulness. And you shall know the Lord. (Hos 2:19–20)

This betrothal, like all of God's promises, finds its fulfillment in Jesus Christ, who spoke of himself as a bridegroom and often compared his kingdom to a wedding feast.[2] He is God's living vow embodying the promise. His bride has not replaced Israel, rather, the borders of Israel have now been extended through the new covenant. No longer a geopolitical nation, limited to one specific ethnic group, it is an international remnant "from every tribe, kindred, and nation" wed to Christ Jesus, the only bridegroom for sinners. Thus, St. Paul could later exhort husbands with the following:

---

[1] Revelation 19:7-9.
[2] Matthew 9:15; 22:1-14.

> Husbands, love your wives, as Christ loved the church and
> gave himself up for her, that he might sanctify her, having
> cleansed her by the washing of water with the word, so that
> he might present the church to himself in splendor, without
> spot or wrinkle or any such thing, that she might be holy and
> without blemish. (Eph 5:25–27)

Holy matrimony is not a human institution, malleable in the
hands of an ever-changing culture. "It is a divine creation,"
writes R.C. Ortlund, "intended to project onto the screen of
human imagination the beauty of a Savior who gives himself
sacrificially for his bride and of his bride who yields herself
gratefully back to him."[3] Husbands are therefore imperfect
examples of the self-sacrificing love of Christ for his church.

Note the one doing all the key verbs in the passage
above: *loved, gave himself, sanctified, cleansed.* This is remarkably counter-cultural. Today, a bride gets herself ready with
the help of close friends, family, and professionals. They
painstakingly pick the dress, hairstyle, make-up, jewelry, and
shoes. But in our marital union with Christ, he beautifies
and styles his own beloved, providing a pure linen dress,
the adornments, and jewelry.[4] As a result, Christ's Church
will be presented beautiful, pure and holy upon his return
to celebrate the marriage feast of the Lamb in his kingdom
that is without end.

A ROYAL MARRIAGE

In his treatise *The Freedom of a Christian*, Martin Luther
says the Gospel is like a wedding vow in which Christ gives

---

[3] R.C. Ortlund, Jr. "Marriage," in *New Dictionary of Biblical Theology* (Downers
Grove, IL: IVP, 2000), 654.

[4] See Isaiah 61:10; Revelation 19:8.

himself to believers.[5] The Gospel is not advice to follow but a Person to trust. It is not merely historical information *about* Jesus but a Word *from* Jesus that changes the reality of those who believe it, just like the vows spoken at a wedding.

As a man and woman stand before their pastor and assembled guests on their wedding day, they make specific promises to God and one another, and in doing so, their marital status is changed. The pastor pronounces them husband and wife, and from that moment forward, their vocations, responsibilities, and relations are forever altered. In like manner, Christ's promise gives what he pledges: forgiveness, life, and salvation.

God justifies sinners by giving us Christ in his promise. Because of the profundity of such a promise, the reformers considered the doctrine of justification to be *the* doctrine by which the Church stands or falls. Unfortunately, many dismiss the importance of this biblical truth because they believe that stressing the forensic nature of God's pardon somehow diminishes the relational dimension of salvation. Such concern is unwarranted. Marriage is also a legal relationship bound by promises spoken but one completely initiated and entrenched in a loving commitment to forsake all others.

Luther said that we cannot truly appreciate this union unless we view it as a "royal marriage." In receiving her heavenly Bridegroom, believers inherit all that is his, including all the things promised through the prophet Hosea: righteousness, justice, love, etc. The flip side of the coin is that Christ inherits all his beloved's sin debts.

It is the greatest rags to riches story in the history of the world. Those who were once prostitutes have become princesses—a royal union! We have been clothed in the righteous gown of our wedded Prince of Peace as he has nailed our sin debt to his cross. Thus, Luther concludes:

---

[5]   LW 31:351–52.

Who can understand the riches of the glory of this grace?
Here this rich and divine bridegroom Christ marries the
poor, wicked harlot, redeems her from all her evil, and adorns
her with all his goodness. Her sins cannot now destroy her,
since they are laid upon Christ and swallowed up by him.
And she has that righteousness in Christ, her husband, of
which she may boast as of her own and which she can confidently display alongside her sins in the face of death and hell
and say, "If I have sinned, yet my Christ, in whom I believe,
has not sinned, and all his is mine and all mine is his," as the
bride in the Song of Solomon says, "My beloved is mine and
I am his" (Song 2:16).[6]

BECOME WHAT YOU ARE

Like most young children, I wore the clothes my parents provided, with little say in the matter. Being frugal, my mother
would often purchase shirts, pants, and shoes a size too big,
knowing that I was still growing. When I would complain
that something didn't fit, she replied with the typical mom
cliché: "You'll grow into them." So it is with the wedding
dress that our Bridegroom provides.

God doesn't wait to pronounce us righteous until we
have cleaned up our act or met some threshold of spiritual
progress. Instead, he justifies us while we are still sinners
(Rom 5:8). And this side of heaven, we are both—simulta-
neously saint and sinner. Thus, we live out our new life in
Christ Jesus by "growing into" the righteous status he has
bestowed by his efficacious promise. The Bible refers to this
as "sanctification."

To be sanctified is to be "set apart" *by* God *for* God.
It is both definitive and developmental. Sanctification is

---

[6]   LW 31:352.

therefore the fruit of being justified. The external declaration of righteousness is complemented with the internal work of the Holy Spirit to become what God has already declared us to be. Gerhard Forde defines this process as "getting used to being justified totally by faith."[7] Said differently, it is coming to grips with being Christ's immortal beloved. "Only God is holy," Forde continues, "and what He says and speaks and does is holy."[8] Therefore, he not only invites us to participate in the eternal life of his kingdom as his bride but grants us a share of his holiness.

It will take a lifetime to get used to being in the royal family when you formerly "walked the streets for money."[9] This privileged position brings a new identity but also new-found expectations. After all, a princess does not behave like a prostitute, nor would she want to.

When we stop to reflect upon the royal nature of our vocation as Christ's bride, we may at times feel a lot of pressure. Our former way of life did not exactly prepare us for this. But if we are not careful, we will soon be tempted to locate the source of our identity in what we do instead of what Christ has already done. When this happens, we are swapping our wedding dress for fig leaves, falling right back into the hole of self-justification by assuming that our worth is measured by our performance.

The encouragement toward holiness in the Bible is always grounded in God's grace, taking the literary form: "Because of this, do that." Scholars refer to this as the *indicatives* and *imperatives* of scriptural ethics. The indicatives tell us what God has done (gospel); the imperatives tell us how

---

[7] Gerhard Forde, *Justification by Faith: A Matter of Life and Death* (Eugene, OR: Wipf and Stock, 2012), 51.

[8] Gerhard Forde, *On Being a Theologian of the Cross: Reflections on Luther's Heidelberg Disputation, 1518* (Grand Rapids, MI: Eerdmans, 1997), 59.

[9] Gordon Matthew Thomas Sumner, 1978. Roxanne. The Police. *Outlandos d'Amour*. [Vinyl]. England: A&M Records.

we should respond (law). For example, St. Peter provides the following indicatives related to God's call:

> But you are a chosen race, a royal priesthood, a holy nation, a people for his own possession, that you may proclaim the excellencies of him who called you out of darkness into his marvelous light. (1 Pet 2:9)

It is only after locating our identity *in Christ* that he brings the imperative:

> Beloved, I urge you as sojourners and exiles to abstain from the passions of the flesh, which wage war against your soul. (1 Pet 2:11)

In other words, darkness signifies our past. We are now people called into his marvelous light. Therefore, we walk as in daylight—open, transparent, unashamed—because we are called to abstain from the kinds of things we once did under the cover of darkness.

Because Christ's beloved has been showered with such undeserved grace and unconditional love, it produces a heart filled with gratitude and reciprocal love. Grace is the foundation of salvation, and gratitude is the category for a virtuous life. In other words, grace begets gratitude.

The nature of this "become what you already are" is remarkably counter-cultural as it defies decades of spiritual self-help messaging. We must be careful readers of the Bible lest we turn the indicatives into imperatives. Our ability to carry out the imperatives of our sanctified life depends entirely on the indicatives of our new status as those who are now Christ's beloved bride.

We do not do what is holy in order to become holy. Rather, we who already *are* holy through faith in Christ will consequently *do* what is holy for the sake of our neighbor. This may sound like something Yoda would say, but it is true nonetheless: holy does as holy is.[10]

Welcome to the wonderful world of being all dressed in the white wedding gown of the world's rightful King.

[10] For an in-depth treatment of this topic in St. Paul's writing, see Paul E. Deterding, *Colossians* (St. Louis: CPH, 2003), 137–60.

Chapter 5

Vestis Virum Facit

The apparel oft proclaims the man.
—Shakespeare

William Shakespeare was not the first to observe our propensity to judge a book by its cover. Writers ancient to modern have put their personal spin on the old proverb: *vestis virum facit* (clothes make the man). For example, in Mark Twain's short story *The Czar's Soliloquy*. a Russian aristocrat looks at his sad naked reflection in a mirror and ponders the nature of his authority apart from his royal apparel. He asks rhetorically, "What is a man without his clothes?"

> One realizes that without his clothes a man would be nothing at all; that the clothes do not merely make the man, the clothes *are* the man; that without them he is a cipher, a vacancy, a nobody, a nothing...There is no power without clothes.[1]

---

[1]   Mark Twain, "The Czar's Soliloquy," *North American Review* 205 (1917): 775–80.

It would be easy to dismiss this as superficial. After all, we have been told that it is what's on the inside that counts, right? It turns out, Twain may have been on to something. Several recent studies have proven the psychological and performative benefits of clothing in daily life.

One study surveyed over five hundred of the world's top companies to assess the impact of dress in the workplace. The findings concluded that continually relaxed dress ultimately leads to relaxed manners, relaxed morals, and relaxed productivity. Swiss Bank, UBS, raised some eyebrows for their legendary forty-four page employee dress code, where they note, "The garment is a critical form of non-verbal communication." So much for casual Fridays!

Two Northwestern University researchers coined the term "enclothed cognition" to describe how clothing systematically influences a wearer's self-understanding based upon the symbolic meaning attached to particular garments. In one study, college students repeatedly scored higher test results when wearing a white lab coat, in contrast to performing the same battery of tests without it. The study's co-author explains that some articles of clothing are rich in symbolism. For example, the robe of a judge signifies justice, an expensive suit signifies power, and a white lab coat signifies attention to detail.[2]

These findings shouldn't come as a complete surprise. Dressing to impress can certainly influence how others see us, but what is perhaps less obvious is how it can affect our self-perception and resultant behavior. The theory is called "symbolic interactionism" in the social sciences. When we surround ourselves with objects that symbolize a particular role, our sense of identity begins to interact with those

---

[2]   Hajo Adam and Adam D. Galinsky, "Enclothed Cognition," *JESP* 48/4 (2012): 918–25.

symbols, and we unconsciously begin to behave in ways we expect a person who wears such clothes to behave.[3]

CRUCIFORMITY

Enclothed cognition is also true of a Christian's self-understanding when we recognize the manner in which God has covered us. Just as justification is a matter of death and life, so, too, is the sanctified life. The two are inseparably linked. It is the daily crucifixion of our old *naked* self in Adam and the rising of our new *clothed* self in Christ. The death of the old comes through the gift of repentance; the resurrection of the new by embracing our identity as God's forgiven children over and over again. Rinse. Repeat. Paul uses the image of taking off and putting on to describe this repentant cycle.[4] We take off our old sin-soiled garments that represent our past life and put on our new clean clothes reflecting the way of the cross.[5]

Though Paul had quite the religious resumé from which to boast, when he self-identifies, he does so as one dead to the law and crucified with Christ:

> For through the law I died to the law, so that I might live to God. I have been crucified with Christ. It is no longer I who live, but Christ who lives in me. And the life I now live in the flesh I live by faith in the Son of God, who loved me and gave himself for me. (Gal 2:19–21)

---

[3] Michael R. Solomon, "The Role of Products as Social Stimuli," *JCR* 10/3 (1983): 319–29.

[4] Martin Luther began his famous 95 theses by noting, "When our Lord and Master Jesus Christ said, 'Repent,' he willed the entire life of believers to be one of repentance."

[5] See Ephesians 4:22-24; Colossians 3:9-10. Catechumens in the early church would take off their old clothes and put on a white robe for the rite of Holy Baptism to show what was happening to them spiritually.

The implication is that before he met the risen Christ, Paul found his worth through works of the law as a zealous Pharisee.[6] His identity was shaped by strict adherence to the law. But now he has "died to the law," which is to say, he has died to it as the means of his salvation. He has been freed from the condemnation of the law as a sinner before God as if he had already died and been judged. Christ's past is now his past; Christ's life is now his life. And this is true of every believer, dear reader, including you.

The cross is not merely one aspect of the Christian life which we accept and then move on from as if there are other more important spiritual endeavors to tackle. Jesus said, "If anyone would come after me, let him deny himself and take up his cross daily and follow me" (Luke 9:23). In other words, our very lives are to be shaped by the cross. To follow Jesus in the way of the cross means to open oneself to the contempt of the world as we strive to love God and neighbor.

Michael Gorman describes this with the word "cruciformity." A cruciform life means that our sense of identity is determined by our relationship to the cross of Christ.[7] The cross is not only the means by which we are saved, but it is also the means by which we truly come to know and trust God. God does not remain hidden and aloof from his creation, but desires to be known exclusively through his crucified Son. As polymath, Blaise Pascal, put it:

> Not only do we know God by Jesus Christ alone, but we know ourselves by Jesus Christ alone. We know life and death by Jesus Christ alone. Apart from Jesus Christ we know not what is our life, nor our death, nor God, nor ourselves.[8]

---

[6]   See Philippians 3:4–6 for Paul's short autobiography.

[7]   Michael Gorman, *Cruciformity: Paul's Narrative Spirituality of the Cross* (Grand Rapids: Eerdmans, 2001), 48-49.

[8]   Blaise Pascal, *The Thoughts of Blaise Pascal* (London: George Bell and Sons, 1905), 224–25.

Luther famously confessed, "The cross alone is our theology," by which he meant that all theology must therefore be crucified. For example, when we confess in the Nicene Creed that we believe in "one God, the Father almighty, maker of heaven and earth," we would not know God as Father from the material creation. It certainly testifies that there is a creator, but that specific divine being remains hidden and nameless as God our Father until he is known in and through his incarnate and crucified Son.[9] Likewise, the "Holy Spirit, the Lord and giver of life," remains unknown and unknowable except in the crucified Son, for it is the Spirit's vocation to "bear witness of" and "glorify Him."[10] Like a spotlight, the Spirit is ever shining his light on Jesus.

When Paul says he has been "crucified with Christ," he is confessing that he no longer has an independent identity apart from that crucified Lord he now follows. This is important to keep in mind since we live in a culture that primarily defines people by their occupation, politics, gender, sexuality, skin color, marital status, or even by how many "likes" or "followers" they have on social media. Such labels serve a limited purpose, but they are not ultimately defining.

As we cling to the cross, we must be prepared to consistently find ourselves at odds with a dying world. As Paul notes, "But far be it from me to boast except in the cross of our Lord Jesus Christ, by which the world has been crucified to me, and I to the world" (Gal 6:14). Nevertheless, in the ups and downs of life, we find our identity secured by the only One who went through death and rose victoriously over it.

---

[9] See Romans 1:20.
[10] See John 14:15–17, 26; 15:26; 16:7–15.

PROTECTIVE CLOTHING

Growing up, I spent a lot of time on job sites with my father, who owned a construction company. Most of his employees wore the clothing brand Carhartt* to work because their materials are made for durability, providing an extra layer of protection against the typical cuts and scrapes that come from hauling lumber and swinging a hammer for a living. Similarly, our identity in Christ means we are protected from even death itself. As part of Paul's correction to the erring Galatians, he reminds them not only who they are but *whose* they are with some key prepositions as a result of being baptized:

> For all of you who were baptized *into* Christ have clothed yourselves *with* Christ. (Gal 3:27, italics mine)

Holy Baptism provides the sin-protective clothing you need—a paradoxical rescue from death—as you have drowned in the flood of Christ's saving grace.[11] Death is a scary reality, of course, which is why billions are spent annually to prevent or delay it from happening. But dying with Christ is *sui generis*, for when you die with him, you also live with him.

> For if we have been united with him in a death like his, we shall certainly be united with him in a resurrection like his. We know that our old self was crucified with him in order that the body of sin might be brought to nothing, so that we would no longer be enslaved to sin. For one who has died has been set free from sin. Now if we have died with Christ, we believe that we will also live with him. (Rom 6:5–8)

---

[11] For an in-depth look on the topic of Holy Baptism, see my book, *Wittenberg vs. Geneva: A Biblical Bout in 7 Rounds on the Doctrines that Divide* (Irvine, CA: New Reformation Publications, 2015), 59–89.

Baptism is a daily reminder of our identity as God's children. We are no longer enslaved to sin but enclothed with Christ's liberating righteousness. Note the present tense refrain of my favorite hymn celebrating this reality: "God's own child, I gladly say it; I *am* baptized into Christ!"[12] Far from being a past tense religious rite with no ongoing benefit, the effects of baptism are eternal. To all appearances, we are the same person as before, but not to our heavenly Father. We have become adopted "sons of God through faith" (Gal 3:26).

Clothes literally "make the man" when they are Christ's clothes. This is true even when we fail to wear his clothes properly on account of our sin. This is objective and comforting good news, particularly when we find ourselves staring into the mirror of own moral failure. Harold Senkbeil notes:

> Looking at my own life I am only too aware of my sin and failure. But as far as God is concerned, my sinful nature is dead and gone. He sees only the new man in Christ—perfect, whole and complete. This is reality but it is a hidden reality... this calls for faith. Our real identity as new men and women in Christ will not be obvious until He comes again. When he appears, then our holiness and worth and value will be apparent to everyone—including us! But not yet. Until then we live by faith, recognizing that the Christian life is a hidden life.[13]

Although we already possess eternal life now, we do not yet experience it in full. For now, is it hidden under and shaped by the cross as we eagerly await this incredible promise: "When Christ who is your life appears, then you also will appear with him in glory" (Col 3:4).

---

[12] Erdmann Neumeister, "God's Own Child, I Gladly Say It," in *Lutheran Service Book* (St. Louis: CPH, 2006), 594.

[13] Harold L. Senkbeil, *Sanctification: Christ in Action* (Milwaukee, WI: Northwestern, 1989), 139–40.

Chapter 6

These Boots Were Made for... Talking?

There's an awful lot you can tell about a person
by their shoes.
—Forrest Gump

I didn't grow up in the Church. Christmas and Easter were celebrated, of course, but these were chiefly secular holidays in my house. I was nineteen and serving in the U.S. Navy when a fellow sailor introduced the Gospel to me. To borrow C.S. Lewis's phrase, I was a "reluctant convert," as I wanted nothing to do with Jesus at that point in my life. To his credit, my shipmate was patiently persistent. He was intelligent without being arrogant. He asked existential questions about truth, life, and meaning. He listened and genuinely cared about me. The fact that I had no credible answers in response to his queries left me feeling rather hollow, and in the end, without any true hope.

As a well-read apologist, he additionally provided me with compelling historical evidence for Christ's life, death, and resurrection in order to validate the Gospel records. On one dark night of the soul, I picked up a Bible he had given me and read through the entire Gospel of John that he had marked with a note that said, "Start here!" Near the end of the fourth gospel, John provides his purpose for writing it:

> Now Jesus did many other signs in the presence of the disciples, which are not written in this book; but these are written so that you may believe that Jesus is the Christ, the Son of God, and that by believing you may have life in his name. (John 20:30–31)

I put the Bible down that night convinced Jesus was, in fact, the Son of God. I was a novice disciple of Christ and found life in his name. I needed a preacher, and God sent me an unexpected and unwanted one. Reflecting back on this sailor and the time he spent preaching Christ crucified to me, I cannot say it better than Paul: "How beautiful are the feet of those who preach good news."[1]

You may not think of feet as being particularly beautiful, unless you have a strange fetish, but when they are shod in the good news of Christ *for you*, they can do both the walking and the talking.

SEEING WITH YOUR EARS?

One of my seminary professors likened the preaching office to that of a pizza deliveryman. He doesn't own the restaurant or make the pizza. He simply delivers it because the

---

[1]   Romans 10:15 (a paraphrase of Isaiah 52:7).

food will be of no good to the hungry customer unless it gets to him.[2]

Likewise, how can you believe in Jesus if you have never heard of him? And how can you hear about Jesus if someone doesn't tell you about him? This was Paul's logic when he argued that "faith comes from hearing, and hearing from the Word of Christ" (Rom 10:17). Forgiveness was achieved by Christ on the cross, but it is not distributed there. The benefits of the cross must come to you through the means God has graciously provided.

Luther was fond of saying that God's Word cannot be without God's people and, conversely, God's people cannot be without God's Word.

> God has come to us in the crucified man Jesus. This is the theology of the Cross. But that crucified God is an offense to all our own expectations and ideas. Therefore, if we want to meet Him, we must leave our own wisdom and experience behind us and listen to that Word, which in God's name and against our reason declares the crucified man to be "God for us."[3]

The Word of God is living and active and because it is God's Word; it always accomplishes that for which he sends it.[4] Long before "speech act theory" came to prominence in linguistic studies, Lutherans described God's Word as a "deed-word," a creative speech act in and of itself. God is the subject doing all the saving verbs through the means of his preached Word.

The most common complaint that pastors in my tradition receive about their preaching is that their sermons

---

[2] Thank you, Dr. Michael Middendorf.

[3] Cited in Regin Prenter, *More About Luther* (Decorah, IA: Luther College, 1958), 2:66.

[4] Isaiah 55:11.

are not very practical. Many have sadly succumbed to the idea that sermons must be about Christian living, so a lot of preaching is geared to scratch this pragmatic itch. Instead of hearing about what God has accomplished through the life, death, and resurrection of Jesus (Gospel), the focus is on the listener and what he or she should be doing for God (Law).

Personally, I find this boring. I don't go to church to hear about myself or, quite frankly, to hear about you. One of the reasons "practical sermons" are so rampant is because we no longer understand what kind of word the Gospel is. "If the Gospel were a theory," writes Phillip Cary, "then it would not be worth much until you put that into practice."[5] In other words, practical application would be the only way to make it "real" in your life. But the Gospel is not a theory to apply; it is a story to believe. It is Good News, not good advice. Thus, Cary concludes:

> It is good news that gladdens the heart, and it changes our hearts precisely by giving us something to be glad about—something we embrace by faith alone, not by *doing* something about it. To be precise, it gives us *someone* to be glad about. For the gospel, being the story of our Lord Jesus Christ, does not give us practical advice or a theory about how to live our lives. It gives us God in the flesh.[6]

---

[5] Phillip Cary, *Good News for Anxious Christians: 10 Practical Things You Don't Have to Do* (Grand Rapids: Brazos Press, 2010), 161.

[6] Ibid., 161.

EXTRAORDINARILY ORDINARY

Since the rise of social media, there has been a growing trend amongst celebrities to be seen "just like us," where they are featured in photos getting coffee at Starbucks, walking their dog, or changing a diaper. Actresses are posting selfies on Instagram sans makeup, with hashtags like #wokeuplikethis or #nomakeupmonday. While they enjoy an extraordinary life, the point is to project the image of a rather ordinary person behind the glamor.

Many feel the same way about the message of the Gospel. It's so ordinary, but the reality is anything but. A baby boy is born to a young, unwed Jewish virgin in the backwoods town of Bethlehem. The boy grows up in a blue-collar home and later gains some attention for his teaching and miracles. He calls completely unqualified men to his inner circle of leadership, and one of them betrays him into the hands of the enemy. Eventually, he is tried as a common criminal by a Roman governor and sentenced to death by means of crucifixion.

It's not exactly the sort of drama and excitement we have come to expect from contemporary films with heroes that seem impervious to bullets. I'm talking about you, John Wick! Even in the first century, Jews found this Good News scandalous, and the Greeks pure foolishness.[7]

Whenever humanity has attempted to understand and relate to God, we have leaned heavily upon two highly deficient means—our reason and experience. As Steven Paulson notes, this goes all the way back to the beginning:

> Adam and Eve were deluded by the serpent into thinking God was jealously hiding something of his own outside the garden, and as an ironic consequence they had to hide themselves from God in the garden. That is, they sought God not

---

[7]   1 Corinthians 1:22ff.

where God wanted to be found, where his word promised blessing, but where God's word of promise was not. They sought God outside his words.[8]

A young boy once asked his pastor, "If God is everywhere, why do I have to go to church?" I'd be surprised if you never asked this yourself. The pastor replied, "The whole atmosphere is filled with water; but when you want to have a drink you have to go to a faucet." His point was that God doesn't just dwell out there somewhere in a galaxy far, far away, but condescends to make himself known in a specific place through his specific means.

On any given Sunday, words from the Bible are read and proclaimed by rather ordinary men. Water, bread, and wine look like those celebrities without makeup and an expensive wardrobe. Ordinary. Yet it is through these very ordinary and unexpected means that our extraordinary King makes his entry for the forgiveness, life, and salvation of sinners like you and me.

God is not playing a game of hide and seek with his grace. Here we find his grace and love locatable, hearable, and tangible. It is here that the Bread of Life feeds our weary souls. It is here that the fountain of God's love pours abundantly to quench our spiritual thirst. According to Luther, the lowliness of the means the Lord uses to distribute the gifts of salvation parallels the humility of his coming in the flesh. In both cases, faith clings to what is heard, not to what is seen.

There's a big difference between this King and other kings. With the latter everything is outward pomp, great and gallant appearance, magnificent air. But not so with Christ….

---

[8]   Steven D. Paulson, "Luther on the Hidden God," *Word & World Vol. XIX, No. 4* (Fall, 1999), 366.

[We] must not trust what our eyes see, but listen to what this King is teaching us in his Word and Sacrament, namely, I poured out my blood to save you from your sins, to rescue you from death and bring you to heaven; to that end I have given you baptism as a gift for the forgiveness of sins, and preach to you unceasingly by word of mouth concerning this treasure, sealing it to you with the Sacrament of my body and blood, so that you need never doubt. True, it seems little and insignificant, that by the washing of water, the Word, and the Sacrament this should all be effected. But don't let your eyes deceive you. At that time, it seemed like a small and insignificant thing for him to come riding on a borrowed donkey and later be crucified, in order to take away sin, death, and hell. No one could tell this by his appearance, but the prophet foretold it, and his work later fulfilled it. Therefore we must simply grasp it with our ears and believe it with our hearts, for our eyes are blind.[9]

Life just has a way of exceeding our expectations, and this continues to be the story of our not-so-ordinary King. The next time you start to feel the Sunday liturgy at your church has lost its luster, take time to remember that the world's Savior is in your midst always doing the unexpected through such ordinary means. And don't forget to give thanks and pray for those who are called to deliver this Good News. Whether their feet are shod with sandals, oxfords, or cowboy boots, they are beautiful!

---

[9]   Martin Luther, *Sermons of Martin Luther: The House Postils* (Grand Rapids: Baker Publishing, 1996), 1:28.

Chapter 7

BDU

The connection between dress and war is not
far to seek; your finest clothes are those you
wear as soldiers.
—Virginia Woolf

There are times in life where basic etiquette calls for dressing
appropriately for the occasion. Weddings, funerals, and gala
events all carry certain expectations.

My wife and I celebrated our anniversary last year
at our favorite restaurant, which not only serves deli-
cious food but has architecture and decor that transport
you back in time so you feel like a character out of an
F. Scott Fitzgerald novel. It's fancy, so you would expect
people to get dressed up in their finest; but alas, we live
in Southern California, where people come to even nice
places in t-shirts, flip flops, and board shorts! At the end
of our meal, the manager surprised us with complimentary
martinis to say thank you for getting dressed up, which

was very generous of her, but also a sad reflection on how casual our culture has become.

I recognize not everyone feels comfortable in suits or gowns, but I mention it because such casualness has a way of slipping into our spiritual lives. The apostle Paul's closing words to the Church of Ephesus sound the alarm to be properly adorned for daily life as a Christian. Why? Because that daily life is a spiritual battlefield. In the words of C.S. Lewis, we live on "enemy-occupied territory."[1]

> Finally, be strong in the Lord and in the strength of his might. Put on the whole armor of God, that you may be able to stand against the schemes of the devil. For we do not wrestle against flesh and blood, but against the rulers, against the authorities, against the cosmic powers over this present darkness, against the spiritual forces of evil in the heavenly places. Therefore take up the whole armor of God, that you may be able to withstand in the evil day, and having done all, to stand firm. (Ephesians 6:10–13)

Wrestling with the devil and the spiritual forces of evil may sound like crazy talk. But as the poet Baudelaire warned, "The devil's first trick is to convince us he doesn't exist."[2] Be warned. He is…very…real.

When I was commissioned as an officer in the U.S. Navy, *The Art of War* was required reading. Though written nearly 2,500 years ago, Sun Tzu offers some relevant advice:

> If you know the enemy and know yourself, you need not fear the result of a hundred battles. If you know yourself but

---

[1]   C.S. Lewis, *Mere Christianity* (New York: Harper Collins, 2001), 46.

[2]   Charles Baudelaire, *Paris Spleen* (New York: New Directions, 1970), 60. Also used by Kevin Spacey's character, Verbal, in the excellent 1995 film, *Unusual Suspects*.

not the enemy, for every victory gained you will also suffer a
defeat. If you know neither the enemy nor yourself, you will
succumb in every battle.[3]

The first priority is to know the enemy. Jesus decisively
defeated Satan on the cross but will not destroy him until
he returns in judgment. Until that day, our struggle with
demonic forces wages on, so we must remain vigilant. Your
baptism into Christ did not put you on the road to "victorious Christian living," as some popular preachers purport.
Quite the opposite.

What you will experience will be more like Jesus, who
immediately after being raised from his baptismal waters
was taken into the wilderness where he was tempted by
Satan's lies in a battle over the truth.[4] Baptism grants you
forgiveness, life, and salvation, but also a very wicked and
crafty foe.

The second thing to know is yourself—requiring in
equal measure honesty and humility—because in this fight,
the devil is an opponent you cannot outmatch on your own.
Luther makes this clear in his beloved hymn:

> The old satanic foe, has sworn to work us woe;
> With craft and dreadful might, he arms himself to fight;
> On earth is not his equal.[5]

The military has physical readiness qualifications to keep its
troops ever-ready to respond, but in this battle it doesn't matter how many push-ups you can do or how far you can run.
When Paul mentions strength, note where it comes from: "Be

[3] Sun Tzu, *The Art of War* (Project Gutenberg e-book, 2005), 36.
[4] See Matthew 4:1–11.
[5] Martin Luther, "A Mighty Fortress is Our God," in *Lutheran Service Book* (St. Louis: CPH, 2006), 657.

strong *in* the Lord and *in* the strength of *his* might." The verb is an imperative passive, *be strengthened*, which means our strength comes not from within but from another. The Lord alone supplies the power to stand firm in this fight against the devil's schemes.

THE FULL ARMOR OF GOD

Having fought in a number of global conflicts during my time on active duty, I had the pleasure of serving alongside the U.S. Marines, who refer to their combat uniforms with the acronym BDU, which stand for "battle dress uniform." Like a good field general, Paul wants us to be properly outfitted for the enlistment we have been called to serve.

This is no time for metaphorical shorts and flip-flops. For this war, we need to be dressed by God himself. Thus, the command, "Put on the whole armor *of* God." Far from being a cheap surplus store find, this is God's own armor.

Keep in mind that Paul was writing this letter from prison, so it's entirely possible that he was staring directly at a Roman soldier as he penned these words. He later refers to himself as an "ambassador in chains" (Eph 6:20). From head to toe, he lists the BDU of a Roman soldier, using this imagery to show how Jesus equips us to fight the good fight.[6]

> Stand therefore, having fastened on the belt of truth, and having put on the breastplate of righteousness, and, as shoes for your feet, having put on the readiness given by the gospel of peace. In all circumstances take up the shield of faith, with which you can extinguish all the flaming darts of the

---

[6] Paul was likely repurposing the "divine warrior" motif of the Old Testament in places like Exodus 15:3, Psalm 18:32–35, and Isaiah 59:9–19.

evil one; and take the helmet of salvation, and the sword of
the Spirit, which is the word of God, praying at all times in
the Spirit, with all prayer and supplication. (Eph 6:14–18)

1. The Belt of Truth

The comparable spiritual belt—the thing upon which everything hangs—is the truth. When Paul talks about the devil's
schemes, he uses the word *methodeias,* meaning his methods
or tactics. The devil attacks not with brute force but with
clever lies, often whispering half truths. From the opening
chapters of Genesis, we have learned that falsehood is his
native tongue. Thus, the most important defensive and offen-
sive weapon in our arsenal is Holy Scripture.

Satan knows that something doesn't need to be true
for it to have devastating effects; it just needs to be believed
and the damage is done. Jesus said that his followers will
know the truth, and the truth will "set them free" (John 8:32).
Trusting in the truth of the Gospel keeps us from being held
captive—a POW behind enemy lines.

2. Breastplate of Righteousness

In order to guard all the vital organs of the body, soldiers
wore a breastplate—the ancient equivalent of a Kevlar vest.
To guard our hearts, we must be covered in Christ's imputed
righteousness. Our righteous deeds offer little help against
the wiles of the devil, so we "put on Christ," trusting that
his righteousness alone qualifies us for heaven and remains
a safeguard to prevent us from doubting God's grace, love,
and acceptance.

3. Gospel Boots

Roman soldiers wore studded sandals that both protected
and anchored their feet in battle, similar to football cleats

today. Rather ironically, he says our combat boots are the "gospel of peace," the Good News of Christ's victory over the great enemies of sin, death, and the devil.

It's hard to fight when you believe it's a lost cause, but here, our victory is sure. We have both peace *with* God and the peace *of* God, so we are bold to proclaim the gospel to all who will hear, for it is the world's only hope as we march through the enemy's territory, enlisting new soldiers along the way. As mentioned in the last chapter, such boots are "beautiful" when they are grounded in and declare "Good News" (Isa 52:7).

4. Shield of Faith

A Roman shield was made of one-inch-thick wood, wrapped in leather and edged with metal. Ancient writers mention "flaming arrows" being used in battle.[7] When the arrows struck and the shield caught fire, Roman soldiers would panic and throw them down, leaving themselves defenseless. Thus, they quickly learned to soak their shields in water before battle so that the arrows would quickly extinguish after hitting their mark.

The spiritual forces of evil will always shoot their flaming arrows of accusation because they don't need a direct hit, just something close to start a fire—the flames of their deceit and temptation—so the surest defense is a shield of faith. Such faith is twofold—the faith once delivered (i.e. the content of what we believe) and our personal faith in the same (trust in Jesus).

---

[7] For example, see Julius Caesar, *The Alexandrian War* (Loeb Classical Library, 1955), 14. Public Domain.

5. Helmet of Salvation

The head is the most vulnerable to attack. If you attempt to go it alone, you're going to take a headshot, so we are to stay under the cover of Christ's salvation. The term "salvation" is an all-encompassing word to describe what God has done to provide our deliverance from sin, death, and the devil. Salvation has three tenses—past, present, and future. I can say, "I have been saved, I am being saved, and I will be saved." But in all cases, it is the Lord who saves. Thus, the saints in heaven clothed in Christ's white robes sing out: "Salvation belongs to the Lord who sits on the throne, and to the Lamb" (Rev 7:10).

6. The Sword of the Spirit

Last but not least, we are called to wield the word of God like a sword. Just as Jesus defended himself from Satan with the assuring phrase, "it is written," so we are to do likewise. With the Word, we parry attacks and riposte the lies of the evil one, knowing that whatever the Word strikes is rendered powerless, for it is sharper than a two-edged sword.

The Greek word used here is not *logos* (word) but *rhema* (message), which emphasizes that we are protected not simply by understanding the Bible intellectually but by proclaiming the very heart of its message in response to doubts, temptations, and sin.

WHERE IS YOUR VICTORY?

Paul ends his battle plan with a plea for persevering prayer. This is battlefield communication with our heavenly HQ. It's simply another way of leaning upon God's strength, wisdom, and truth. And this prayer is a supplication "for all the saints." In other words, there is strength in numbers. We need each other in this fight against the flesh, the world, and the devil. This is no solitary mission; you need your church, and your church needs you. C.S. Lewis said that when we go to church, we are listening in to the secret wireless from our friends, which is why the enemy is so anxious to prevent us from going.[8]

When the Roman Emperor Trajan was on the field of battle, he would take off his own armor and place it on his wounded men. If necessary, he would shred his own garments and use them as bandages. He gained the respect of his men by leading from the front lines.[9]

While certainly noble, this does not even begin to compare to Jesus. He entered the battlefield and willingly gave his very life to defeat your enemies. It looked to the world like a foolish strategy, until the third day. When he rose from the dead, he surprised everyone, including the devil, because the last enemy to overcome is death and that, dear reader, has been conquered, too.

> Death is swallowed up in victory.
> "O death, where is your victory?
> O death, where is your sting?"
>
> The sting of death is sin, and the power of sin is the law.
> But thanks be to God, who gives us the victory through
> our Lord Jesus Christ. (1 Cor 15:54–57)

There is no need to fear the enemy while adorned in this armor because Jesus wore it himself and has risen from the dead and ascended in glory, proving its effectiveness. But

---

[8]   C.S. Lewis, *Mere Christianity*, 46.

[9]   See Nicholas Jackson, *Trajan: Rome's Last Conqueror* (Yorkshire, Green Hill Books, 2022), chapter 7.

note carefully. Wearing this armor is not about becoming more like Jesus in order to defeat Satan but about staying secure in his already finished triumph. Stand firm! Wear Christ's BDUs proudly and confidently.

Chapter 8

Who are You Wearing?

> Life is a party. Dress for it.
> —Audrey Hepburn

"Who are your wearing?" is the question most commonly asked of celebrities when they walk the red carpets of galas, premieres, and awards shows. Behind these stars stands an unseen stylist, a professional who works very hard to ensure their clientele look their fashionable best when the cameras roll. Image is everything in Hollywood, so no expense is spared when it comes to creating and projecting the right persona necessary to sustain relevance in the banality of popular culture.

The rich and famous rely upon stylists for the same reason I consult my wife on my appearance before leaving the house. She will speak the truth in love. We do not always have a very good track record when we look in the mirror and self-evaluate. In fact, the results are often disastrous. Remember Bjork's infamous 2001 Academy Awards swan dress? Knowledgeable, unbiased, and objective eyes are necessary to tell us what we need to hear, let alone wear, even if we do not always like what they have to say.

Far from being superficial, the question, "Who are you wearing?" has eternal consequences when God is the one asking. Welcome to the divine red carpet.

ROYAL FASHION POLICE

During holy week, Jesus told a parable comparing the kingdom of God to a wedding party thrown in honor of a king's son (Matt 22:1–14). The kingdom's A-listers were invited, but as the RSVP's came in, it was painfully clear they had other plans. The king sent his servants with a personal reminder on the day of the wedding: "The ribeyes are on the grill and the Bordeaux is decanting. The feast is ready. Come to the feast!"

Some made lame excuses that were clearly meant to insult; others violently mistreated the king's messengers, even to the point of murder. A royal invitation is the equivalent of a command, so their defiance dishonored the royal family. The king responded swiftly by sending his soldiers to deal with the insubordinate murderers.

Despite their refusal, the wedding feast was ready, and a party must have guests to celebrate, so the king invited everyone else—the good, the bad, and the ugly. They didn't deserve to be at such a lavish affair, but such was the king's generosity and desire to see his son honored. Since people from all walks of life were included with little time to prepare, the king provided them with attire appropriate for the occasion. They served as concealment of the guests' socio-economic status. Everyone present was there solely at the king's invitation and appropriately adorned to celebrate his son's matrimony.

As the king surveyed the crowd enjoying his extravagance, one guest stood out, and not in a good way. "Friend, how did you get in here without a wedding garment?" (Matt 22:12). All were invited, but proper dress was still expected, especially since it was generously provided at no cost. The king's question provided an opportunity for the man to confess and be absolved for his fashion faux pas, but the man remained speechless. As celebrity stylist Rachel Zöe says, "Style is a way to say who you are without having to speak." This man's style spoke volumes, even if he would not answer the king. He certainly knew the wedding garments were expected, but he preferred to be there on his own terms. Bad idea! The king had him ejected from the party, where he was barred from re-entry.

This parable is a part of a seven-hundred-year old conversation that began in Isaiah, where the prophet spoke of a great banquet to be held at the end of history. It is depicted as *the* party to end all parties, with God serving the finest food and wine imaginable. The guest list includes people from all nations as God hosts them on his holy hill. There will be no death, tears, or fears in this place. It will be a glorious day of celebration and the consummation of all that God had promised. When this party begins, people will say, "This is the Lord; we have waited for him; let us be glad and rejoice in his salvation" (Isa 25:9).

As Jesus puts his own divine stamp on this prophecy, the point of the parable is clear. The Gospel invitation goes out to all—to the least, the last, and the lost. Israel was invited first to the party, but now the guestlist includes everyone else. No one deserves to be in God's holy palace and presence; nevertheless, the Father is going to fill his heavenly wedding hall on the last day as his Son celebrates and consummates his marriage. There will be rejoicing in his salvation.

But like the man in the parable, you cannot expect to stroll through the pearly gates in the spiritual equivalent of cutoff jeans shorts and not raise some eyebrows. Contrary to a lot of popular self-help preaching, heaven is not a "come as you are" affair. God loves you too much for that, so much so that he has provided the wedding garments of his Son's cross-earned righteousness to wear in faith. In Christ alone you have all that is required. Nothing more is necessary but nothing less is acceptable.

The man without the wedding garment remained speechless, because there was not one good reason to justify his refusal of the king's wardrobe. The point is that hell remains radically unnecessary. As Robert Farrar Capon notes, "there will never be *any reasons*, from God's point of view, for anyone to end up there, precisely because God in Jesus has made his grace, and not our track record, the sole basis of salvation."[1]

In one of my favorite episodes of the sitcom *Friends,* Ross gets Joey a job as a tour guide at the Natural History Museum. Joey quickly learns that there is an employee hierarchy represented by the kind of coat you wear. When he attempts to save a seat for Ross in the cafeteria at lunch, a fellow tour guide named Ronda informs him that Dr. Geller wears a white lab coat, and the white lab coats do not sit with the blue blazer-wearing tour guides.

"How come?," Joey asks.

"That's just the way it is!," Ronda notes.

Perturbed by this notion, he responds, "That's crazy."

"That's crazy in a perfect world, a world without lab coats and blazers," Ronda exclaims, "but you're not in a perfect world!"

When Ross finally arrives, he awkwardly turns down Joey's offer and sits with his fellow white coats as Ronda

---

[1]   Robert Farrar Capon, *Kingdom, Grace, Judgement: Paradox, Outrage, and Vindication in the Parables of Jesus* (Grand Rapids: Eerdmans, 2002), 462.

predicted. Convicted of his lunch time segregation, the next day, Ross enters and offers a cafeteria confession: "We work in a natural history museum, and yet, there is something… unnatural…about the way we eat lunch."[2]

The episode comically captures how something as superficial as a jacket can divide us. As I have noted throughout this little book, what separates us from God and one another is sin. What ultimately reconciles us with God and one another is Jesus Christ. And this, too, is represented by the clothing worn by those who have departed this imperfect world.

LAUNDRY DAY

Unless you suffer from some obsessive-compulsive disorder, I doubt you enjoy doing laundry. But in his vision of heaven, John notes a paradoxical truth about the saints' clothing. He sees an innumerable multitude from every nation gathered around the throne of the Lamb, dressed in white robes and singing: "Salvation belongs to our God who sits on the throne, and to the Lamb" (Rev 7:10).

After John is questioned about the identity of this white-robed choir and where they come from, we learn, "These are the ones coming out of the great tribulation. They have washed their robes and made them white in the blood of the Lamb" (Rev 7:14). The present participle in the phrase, "coming out of," suggests believers are continually emerging from their earthly tribulation, adding to this diverse heavenly crowd. They have come from this present vale of tears—a time of trial and testing—having passed through death to life. As Louis Brighton notes, "John is looking at the church in its eschatological state, which state the souls of all Christians

---

[2]   David Crane, Marta Kaufmann, and Seth Kurland, "The One with Phoebe's Uterus," episode, *Friends* (NBC, January 8, 1998).

enter the moment of their death and which is consummated at the resurrection of the body and the End."[3]

This diverse crowd is united by wearing the white wedding garments of the Son, graciously provided by the Father as a gift. Sound familiar? It should. The color white signifies purity before God's holy eyes. The saints, as Rod Rosenbladt has often said, are those who have bet all their chips on Jesus Christ, trusting in his shed blood for the atonement of their sins.

Blood isn't the first cleansing agent that comes to mind when you want to do your laundry; in fact, if you've ever bled on a white shirt and attempted to get the stain out, you know it's no easy task. But when it comes to a cleansing from sin, Christ's blood is a divine detergent that works.[4] The saints in heaven are no longer defined by their former sin and suffering in the Church Militant, but by what Christ has accomplished on the cross for them. They now rest secure in the Church Triumphant, adding their voices to the liturgy of heaven as they are united together in the Lamb.

Yves Saint Laurent once said, "Fashions fade, style is eternal." When you arrive at the doors of heaven and someone asks, "Who are you wearing?," tell them, "Jesus!" God's judgment is the only one that matters, and the Good News is that Christ's white robes will remain eternally fashionable in every age.

From Genesis to Revelation, from the very beginning until the very end, we have traced the golden thread of God's promises to be entirely woven around Jesus Christ. To him be all glory and honor.

---

[3]   Louis A. Brighton, *Revelation* (St. Louis: CPH, 1999), 200.
[4]   See also 1 John 1:7.

1517.

Never Go Another Day Without Hearing the Gospel of Jesus.

Visit **www.1517.org**
for free Gospel resources.